# 365 Positive Thinking Quotes:

*Daily Inspiration Quotes to Get Perked Up without Coffee*

*Ben L Orchard*

# Table of Contents

Description ............................................................. 5

Introduction .......................................................... 6

Chapter 1: 365 Quotes ....................................... 7

Conclusion .......................................................... 68

Additionally, the information in the following pages is intended only for informational purposes and should thus be thought of as universal. As befitting its nature, it is presented without assurance regarding its prolonged validity or interim quality. Trademarks that are mentioned are done without written consent and can in no way be considered an endorsement from the trademark holder.

# Description

Everyone needs a little motivation to get through their day so that they can have a better day. Having that motivation means that you can push through your day no matter how hard it is.

On top of that, motivation helps you to do the tough things in your day. Sometimes, you find that you need just that little extra boost to get started on something that you have been dreading to start.

Taking your life one day at a time and adding a sprinkle of positive to the start of your day will help to change your life in a positive way. You do not need to search quote after quote to help you.

Go through this day one day at a time and you will be able to make it through your day!

# Introduction

Congratulations on downloading 365 Positive Thinking Quotes and thank you for doing so.

The following chapter will provide you with one quote a day to help you get started going through your day without having to hit the coffee pot to wake up.
Each quote will set a positive tone for your day and help you to motivate yourself to have a great day that is not going to rely on anyone else. By the end of the year, you will have started every day positive and hopefully, you see a change in yourself and how your day progresses!

There are plenty of books on this subject on the market, so thanks again for choosing this one! Every effort was made to ensure it is full of as much useful information as possible. Please enjoy!

# Chapter 1: 365 Quotes

**1.**

"When you fail, that is when you get closer to success." - Stephen Richards

**2.**

"In order to succeed, your desire for success should be greater than your fear of failure." - Bill Cosby

**3.**

"People take different roads seeking fulfillment and happiness. Just because they're not on your road doesn't mean they've gotten lost." - Dalai Lama

**4.**

"This is my wish for you: comfort on difficult days, smiles when sadness intrudes, rainbows to follow the clouds, laughter to kiss your lips, sunsets to warm your heart, hugs when spirits sag, beauty for your eyes to see, friendships to brighten your being, faith so that you can believe, confidence for when you doubt, courage to know yourself, patience to accept the truth, love to complete your life." - Anonymous

**5.**

"We do not get to choose how we start out our life. We do not get to choose the day we are born or the family we are born into, what we are named at birth, what country we are born in, and we do not get to choose our ancestry. All these things are predetermined by a higher power. By the time you are old enough to start making decisions for yourself, a lot of things in your life are already in place. It's important, therefore, that you focus on the future, the only thing that you can change." - Idowu Koyenikan

**6.**

"Efforts and courage are not enough without purpose and direction."  - John F. Kennedy

**7.**

"Success comes from the inside out. In order to change what is on the outside, you must first change what is on the inside." - Idowu Koyenikan

**8.**

"Challenges are what make life interesting and overcoming them is what makes life meaningful."- Joshua J. Marine

**9.**

"Once we believe in ourselves, we can risk curiosity, wonder, spontaneous delight, or any experience that reveals the human spirit." - E.E. Cummings

**10.**

"We've all got both light and dark inside us. What matters is the part we choose to act on. That's who we really are." - J. K. Rowling

**11.**

"You don't have the power to make life "fair," but you do have the power to make life joyful." - Jonathan Lockwood Huie

**12.**

"Whatever you want in life, start today. Not tomorrow – today. Let it be a small beginning – a tiny beginning. Your happiness depends on starting today – every day." - Jonathan Lockwood Huie

**13.**

"People will, in a great degree and not without reason, form their opinion of you upon that which they have of your friends; and there is a Spanish proverb which says very justly, "Tell me whom you live with, and I will tell you who you are." - Lord Chesterfield

**14.**

"The only way to do great work is to love what you do. If you haven't found it yet, keep looking. Don't settle." - Steve Jobs

**15.**

"Start living now. Stop saving the good china for that special occasion. Stop withholding your love until that special person materializes. Every day you are alive is a special occasion. Every minute, every breath, is a gift from God." - Mary Manin Morrissey.

**16.**

"Nothing can stop the man with the right mental attitude from achieving his goal; nothing on earth can help the man with the wrong mental attitude." - Thomas Jefferson

**17.**

"Optimism is the faith that leads to achievement. Nothing can be done without hope and confidence." - Helen Keller

**18.**

"Courage doesn't always roar. Sometimes courage is the quiet voice at the end of the day saying, "I will try again tomorrow." - Mary Anne Radmacher

**19.**

"Consult not your fears but your hopes and your dreams. Think not about your frustrations, but about your unfulfilled potential. Concern yourself not with what you tried and failed in, but with what it is still possible for you to do." - Pope John XXIII

**20.**

"You are not here merely to make a living. You are here in order to enable the world to live more amply, with greater vision, with a finer spirit of hope and achievement. You are here to enrich the world, and you impoverish yourself if you forget the errand." - Woodrow Wilson

**21.**

"Be impeccable with your words. Speak with integrity. Say only what you mean. Avoid using the word to speak against yourself or to gossip about others. Use the power of your word in the direction of truth and love."- Don Miguel Ruiz

**22.**

"Live to experience something new each day – to learn something new, to meet a new friend, to bring joy into someone's life, to feel the wind newly on your skin, to touch a new fear and a new anger, and with focused intent and good fortune, to find an ample measure of your own joy." - Jonathan Lockwood Huie

**23.**

"Our prime purpose in this life is to help others. And if you can't help them, at least don't hurt them." - Tenzin Gyatso, the 14th Dalai Lama

**24.**

"The way to get started is to quit talking and begin doing." - Walt Disney

**25.**

"Being defeated is often a temporary condition. Giving up is what makes it permanent." - Marilyn vos Savant

**26.**

"You learn more from failure than from success. Don't let it stop you. Failure builds character." - Unknown

**27.**

"You may be disappointed if you fail, but you are doomed if you don't try." - Beverly Sills

**28.**

"Courage is the greatest of all virtues, because if you don't have courage, you may not have an opportunity to use any of the others." - Samuel Johnson

**29.**

"By recording your dreams and goals on paper, you set in motion the process of becoming the person you most want to be. Put your future in good hands - your own."–Mark Victor Hansen

**30.**

"Treat those who are good with goodness, and also treat those who are not good with goodness. Thus goodness is attained. Be honest to those who are honest, and be also honest to those who are not honest. Thus honesty is attained." - Lao Tzu

**31.**

"You cannot cross the sea merely by standing and staring at the water." - Rabindranath Tagore

**32.**

"I think goals should never be easy. They should force you to work, even if they are uncomfortable at the time." - Michael Phelps

**33.**

"Things work out best for those who make the best of how things work out." - John Wooden

**34.**

"Today's accomplishments were yesterday's impossibilities." - Robert H. Schuller

**35.**

"Teach your children early not to pass the blame or make excuses, but to take responsibility for their actions." - Eric Greitens

**36.**

"Happiness is not something readymade. It comes from your own actions." - Dalai Lama

**37.**

"Life is about making an impact, not making an income." - Kevin Kruse

**38.**

"I attribute my success to this: I never gave or took any excuse." - Florence Nightingale

**39.**

"Limitations live only in our minds. But if we use our imaginations, our possibilities become limitless." - Jamie Paolinetti

**40.**

"Never be ashamed! There's some who will hold it against you, but they are not worth bothering with." - J. K. Rowling

**41.**

"If we did all the things we are capable of, we would literally astound ourselves." - Thomas Edison

**42.**

"The mind is everything. What you think you become." - Buddha

**43.**

"The most common way people give up their power is by thinking they don't have any." - Alice Walker

**44.**

"Every tomorrow has two handles. We can take hold of it with the handle of anxiety or the handle of faith." - Henry Ward Beecher

**45.**

"Darkness cannot drive out darkness; only light can do that. Hate cannot drive out hate; only love can do that." - Martin Luther King Jr.

**46.**

"Eighty percent of success is showing up." - Woody Allen

**47.**

"The only time you fail is when you fall down and stay down." - Stephen Richards

**48.**

"You can never cross the ocean until you have the courage to lose sight of the shore." - Christopher Columbus

**49.**

"The two most important days in your life are the day you are born and the day you find out why"- Mark Twain

**50.**

"Destiny is not a matter of chance, it is a matter of choice. It is not a thing to be waited for, it is a thing to be achieved." - William Jennings Bryan

**51.**

"Failure will never overtake me if my determination to succeed is strong enough." - Og Mandino

**52.**

"Your voice can change the world." - Barack Obama

**53.**

"Believe you can and you're halfway there." - Theodore Roosevelt

**54.**

"A creative man is motivated by the desire to achieve, not by the desire to beat others." - Ayn Rand

**55.**

"When one door of happiness closes, another opens, but often, we look so long at the closed door that we

do not see the one that has been opened for us." -
Helen Keller

**56.**

"Once you replace negative thoughts with positive
ones, you'll start having positive results." - Willie
Nelson

**57.**

"First, have a definite, clear practical ideal; a goal, an
objective. Second, have the necessary means to
achieve your ends; wisdom, money, materials, and
methods. Third, adjust all your means to that end." -
Aristotle

**58.**

"You can't fall if you don't climb. But there's no joy in living your whole life on the ground." - Unknown

**59.**

"If the wind will not serve, take to the oars." - Latin Proverb

**60.**

"We must believe that we are gifted for something, and that this thing, at whatever cost, must be attained." - Marie Curie

**61.**

"Winning isn't everything, but wanting to win is." - Vince Lombardi

**62.**

"Be yourself; everyone else is taken." - Oscar Wilde

**63.**

"I am not a product of my circumstances. I am a product of my decisions." - Stephen Covey

**64.**

"Successful people have fear, successful people have doubts, and successful people have worries. They just don't let these feelings stop them." - T. Harv Eker

**65.**

"Always be a first-rate version of yourself instead of a second-rate version of somebody else." - Judy Garland

**66.**

"The person who says it cannot be done should not interrupt the person who is doing it." - Chinese Proverb

**67.**

"A person who never made a mistake never tried anything new." - Albert Einstein

**68.**

"Build your own dreams, or someone else will hire you to build theirs." - Farrah Gray

**69.**

"It does not matter how slowly you go as long as you do not stop." - Confucius

**70.**

"Do what you can, where you are, with what you have." - Teddy Roosevelt

**71.**

"The successful warrior is the average man, with laser-like focus." - Bruce Lee

**72.**

"Education is the most powerful weapon which you can use to change the world." - Nelson Mandela

**73.**

"Without leaps of imagination or dreaming, we lose the excitement of possibilities. Dreaming, after all, is a form of planning." - Gloria Steinem

**74.**

"If you do what you've always done, you'll get what you've always gotten." - Tony Robbins

**75.**

"I have been impressed with the urgency of doing. Knowing is not enough; we must apply. Being willing is not enough; we must do." - Leonardo da Vinci

**76.**

"Life is what we make it, always has been, always will be." - Grandma Moses

**77.**

"When everything seems to be going against you, remember that the airplane takes off against the wind, not with it." - Henry Ford

**78.**

"Yesterday is dead. Tomorrow is a dream. Today – each today – is where the action is – where all of life occurs. Today is your life – your only life. Live today to the fullest." - Jonathan Lockwood Huie

**79.**

"Keep your thoughts positive because your thoughts become your words. Keep your words positive because your words become your behavior. Keep your behavior positive because your behavior becomes your habits. Keep your habits positive because your habits become your values. Keep your values positive because your values become your destiny." - Mahatma Gandhi

**80.**

"At the end of the day, let there be no excuses, no explanations, no regrets."
- Dr. Steve Maraboli

**81.**

"The greatest danger for most of us is not that our aim is too high and we miss it, but that it is too low and we reach it." - Michelangelo

**82.**

"In the real world, the smartest people are people who make mistakes and learn. In school, the smartest people don't make mistakes." - Robert Kiyosaki

**83.**

"If you have no critics, you'll likely have no success." - Malcolm Forbes

**84.**

"Always choose the future over the past. What do we do now?" - Brian Tracy

**85.**

"Life is either a great adventure or nothing at all." - Helen Keller

**86.**

"Dreaming, after all, is a form of planning." - Gloria Steinem

**87.**

"The best preparation for tomorrow is doing your best today." - H. Jackson Brown Jr.

**88.**

"The best way to find yourself is to lose yourself in the service of others." - Mohandas K. Gandhi

**89.**

"The jump is so frightening between where I am and where I want to be. Because of all I may become, I close my eyes and leap." - Mary Anne Radmacher

**90.**

"Whether you be man or woman, you will never do anything in this world without courage. It is the greatest quality of the mind next to honor."- James Lane Allen

**91.**

"It is not the strongest of the species that survive, nor the most intelligent, but the one most responsive to change." - Charles Darwin

**92.**

"It takes as much energy to wish as it does to plan."- Eleanor Roosevelt

**93.**

"There's a tremendous bias against taking risks. Everyone is trying to optimize their ass-covering." - Elon Musk

**94.**

"Please think about your legacy, because you're writing it every day." -Gary Vaynerchuck

**95.**

"It is never too later to be what you might have been."- George Eliot

**96.**

"The time is always right to do what is right." - Martin Luther King Jr.

**97.**

"Desire is the key to motivation, but its determination and commitment to an unrelenting pursuit of your goal - a commitment to excellence - that will enable you to attain the success you seek."– Mario Andretti

**98.**

"Either you run the day, or the day runs you." - Jim Rohn

**99.**

"Would you like me to give you a formula for success? It's quite simple, really. Double your rate of failure. You are thinking of failure as the enemy of success. But it isn't at all. You can be discouraged by failure or you can learn from it. So, go ahead and make mistakes. Make all you can. Because remember that's where you will find success."— Thomas J. Watson

**100.**

"Life is a great and wondrous mystery and the only thing we know that we have for sure is what is right here right now. Don't miss it." - Leo Buscaglia

**101.**

"Accept the challenges so that you can feel the exhilaration of victory." - George S. Patton

**102.**

"One finds limits by pushing them."- Herbert Simon

**103.**

"Nothing in life is to be feared, it is only to be understood. Now is the time to understand more, so that we may fear less." - Marie Curie

**104.**

"Trust yourself. Create the kind of self that you will be happy to live with all your life. Make the most of yourself by fanning the tiny inner sparks of possibility into flames of achievement." - Golda Meir

**105.**

"You may be the only person left who believes in you, but it's enough. It takes just one star to pierce a universe of darkness. Never give up." - Richelle E. Goodrich

**106.**

"Everyone has inside of her a piece of good news. The good news is that you don't know how great you can be, how much you can love, what you can accomplish, and what your potential is." - Anne Frank

**107.**

"Every great dreams begins with a dreamer. Always remember, you have within you the strength, the patience, and the passion to reach for the stars to change the world." - Harriet Tubman

**108.**

"I honestly think it is better to be a failure at something you love than to be a success at something you hate." - George Burns

**109.**

"It takes 20 years to build a reputation and five minutes to ruin it. If you think about that, you'll do things differently." - Warren Buffett

**110.**

"Success is empty if you arrive at the finish line alone. The best reward is to get there surrounded by winners." - Howard Schultz

**111.**

"Instead of looking at the past, I put myself ahead twenty years and try to look at what I need to do now in order to get there then." - Diana Ross

**112.**

"Don't wait until everything is just right. It will never be perfect. There will always be challenges, obstacles, and less than perfect conditions. So what? Get started now. With each step you take, you will grow stronger and stronger, more and more skilled, more and more self-confident, and more and more successful." - Mark Victor Hansen

**113.**

"Don't judge each day by the harvest you reap but by the seeds that you plant." - Robert Louis Stevenson

**114.**

"You can't knock on opportunity's door and not be ready." - Bruno Mars

**115.**

"I knew that if I failed I wouldn't regret that, but I knew the one thing I might regret is not trying." - Jeff Bezos

**116.**

"You are never too old to set another goal or to dream a new dream."- C. S. Lewis

**117.**

"Embrace what you don't know, especially in the beginning, because what you don't know can become your greatest asset. It ensures that you will absolutely be doing things different from everybody else." - Sara Blakely

**118.**

"It doesn't matter how far you might rise. At some point, you are bound to stumble. If you're constantly pushing yourself higher, the law of averages, not to mention the Myth of Icarus, predicts that you will at some point fall. And when you do, I want you to know this, remember this: there is no such thing as failure. Failure is just life trying to move us in another direction." - Oprah Winfrey

**119.**

"Don't let yesterday take up too much of today." - Will Rogers

**120.**

"If you steadfastly refuse to quit, you rapidly narrow your options to only winning." - Brad Thor

**121.**

"I've learned that people will forget what you said, people will forget what you did, but people will never forget how you made them feel." - Maya Angelou

**122.**

"Leadership is the art of getting someone else to do something you want done because he wants to do it." - Dwight Eisenhower

**123.**

"To be yourself in a world that is constantly trying to make you something else is the greatest accomplishment." - Ralph Waldo Emerson

**124.**

"Dwell on the beauty of life. Watch the stars, and see yourself running with them." - Marcus Aurelius

**125.**

"Whatever the mind of man can conceive and believe, it can achieve." - Napoleon Hill

**126.**

"Start by doing what's necessary; then do what's possible; and suddenly, you are doing the impossible."
- Francis of Assisi

**127.**

"The only place where success comes before work is in the dictionary." - Vidal Sassoon

**128.**

"There are two types of people who will tell you that you cannot make a difference in this world: those who are afraid to try and those who are afraid you will succeed." - Ray Goforth

**129.**

"Change your thoughts and you change your world."- Norman Vincent Peale

**130.**

"Our greatest glory is not in never failing, but in rising every time we fall." - Confucius

**131.**

"Go confidently in the direction of your dreams. Live the life you have imagined." - Henry David Thoreau

**132.**

"Whatever you can do, or dream you can, begin it. Boldness has genius, power, and magic in it." - Johann Wolfgang von Goethe

**133.**

"Opportunities multiply as they are seized." - Sun Tzu

**134.**

"You're not going to get very far in life based on what you already know. You're going to advance in life by what you're going to learn after you leave here." - Charlie Munger

**135.**

"Dream big and dare to fail." - Norman Vaughan

**136**

"Even if you're on the right track, you'll get run over if you just sit there." - Will Rogers

**137.**

"Don't be afraid to give up the good to go for the great." - John. D Rockefeller

**138.**

"There is nothing impossible to him who will try." - Alexander the Great

**139.**

"Always bear in mind that your own resolution to succeed is more important than any other one thing." - President Abraham Lincoln

**140.**

"Every noble work is at first impossible." - Thomas Carlyle

**141.**

"It takes a great deal of courage to stand up to your enemies, but even more to stand up to your friends." - J. K. Rowling

**142.**

"To understand the heart and mind of a person, look not at what he has already achieved, but what he aspires to do." - Kahlil Gibran

**143.**

"I wish I could tell you the secret to being forever young, but no one's figured that out yet. But if you see the glass half full, simplify your life, and give yourself to a worthy cause, you will be forever happy." - Bert Jacobs

**144.**

"Keep your face always toward the sunshine – and shadows will fall behind you." - Walt Whitman

**145.**

"You have it easily in your power to increase the sum total of this world's happiness now. How? By giving a few words of sincere appreciation to someone who is lonely or discouraged. Perhaps, you will forget tomorrow the kind words you say today, but the recipient may cherish them over a lifetime." - Dale Carnegie

**146.**

"Believe in yourself! Have faith in your abilities! Without a humble but reasonable confidence in your own powers, you cannot be successful or happy." - Norman Vincent Peale

**147.**

"Life has two rules: #1 Never quit; #2 Always remember rule #1." - Unknown

**148.**

"I don't know what your destiny will be, but one thing I know: The only ones among you who will be truly happy are those who have sought and found how to serve." - Albert Schweitzer

**149.**

"Some people are always grumbling because roses have thorns; I am thankful that thorns have roses." - Alphonse Karr

**150.**

"Your present circumstances don't determine where you can go; they merely determine where you start." - Nido Qubein

**151.**

"The greatest leader is not necessarily the one who does the greatest things. He is the one that gets the people to do the greatest things." - Ronald Reagan

**152.**

"Every truth passes through three stages before it is recognized. In the first, it is ridiculed. In the second, it is opposed. In the third, it is regarded as self-evident." - Arthur Schopenhauer

**154.**

"High sentiments always win in the end. The leaders who offer blood, toil, tears, and sweat always get more out of their followers than those who offer safety and a good time. When it comes to the pinch, human beings are heroic."--George Orwell

**155.**

"The reward of a thing well done is having done it." - Ralph Waldo Emerson

**156.**

"Strive not to be a success, but rather to be of value." - Albert Einstein

**157.**

"All you need is the plan, the road map, and the courage to press on to your destination." - Earl Nightingale

**158.**

"If something is important enough, even if the odds are against you, you should still do it." - Elon Musk

**159.**

"It's your place in the world; it's your life. Go on and do all you can with it, and make it the life you want to live." - Mae Jemison

**160.**

"Surviving a failure gives you more self-confidence. Failures are great learning tools...but they must be kept to a minimum." - Jeffrey Immelt

**161.**

"The question isn't who's going to let me; it's who's going to stop me." - Ayn Rand

**162.**

"A good criterion for measuring success in life is the number of people you have made happy." - Robert J Lumsden

**163.**

"Somewhere, something incredible is waiting to be known." - Sharon Begley

**164.**

"Buckle up, and know that it's going to be a tremendous amount of work, but embrace it." - Tory Burch

**165.**

"There's no shortage of remarkable ideas, what's missing is the will to execute them." - Seth Godin

**166.**

"Think left and think right and think low and think high. Oh, the thinks you can think up if only you try." – Dr. Seuss

**167.**

"A leader is one who knows the way, goes the way, and shows the way." - John C. Maxwell

**168.**

"Follow your bliss and the universe will open doors where there were only walls."- Joseph Campbell

**169.**

"Life is 10% what happens to us and 90% how we react to it." - Dennis P Kimbro

**170.**

"Be patient with yourself. Self-growth is tender; it's holy ground. There's no greater investment."-- Stephen Covey

**171.**

"The secret of getting ahead is getting started. The secret of getting started is breaking your complex, overwhelming tasks into smaller manageable tasks, and then starting on the first one." - Mark Twain

**172.**

"You can, you should, and if you're brave enough to start, you will." - Stephen King

**173.**

"It is better to fail in originality than to succeed in imitation" - Herman Melville

**174.**

"Unless you dream, you're not going to achieve anything."- Richard Branson

**175.**

"It's hard to beat a person who never gives up." - Babe Ruth

**176.**

"Greatness is sifted through the grind, therefore, don't despise the hard work now for surely it will be worth it in the end." - Sanjo Jendayi

**177.**

"I'm a greater believer in luck, and I find the harder I work, the more I have it." - Thomas Jefferson

**178.**

"My grandfather once told me that there were two kinds of people: those who do the work and those who take the credit. He told me to try and be in the first group; there was much less competition." -Indira Gandhi

**179.**

"Calm in chaos. In the midst of the flurry – clarity. In the midst of the storm – calm. In the midst of divided interests – certainty. In the many roads – a certain choice." - Mary Anne Radmacher

**180.**

"Hard work helps. It has never killed anyone."- Unknown

**181.**

"No great achiever – even those who made it seem easy – ever succeeded without hard work" - Jonathan Sacks

**182.**

"Nobody's a natural. You work hard to get good and then work to get better. It's hard to stay on top." - Paul Coffey

**183.**

"To be a champ, you have to believe in yourself when no one else will." - Sugar Ray Robinson

**184.**

"The difference between ordinary and extraordinary is that little extra." - Jimmy Johnson

**185.**

"Talent means nothing, while experience, acquired in humility and with hard work, means everything." - Patrick Suskind

**186.**

"All growth depends upon activity. There is no development physically or intellectually without effort, and effort means work." - Calvin Coolidge

**187.**

"Patience can be bitter but her fruit is always sweet." - Habeeb Akande

**188.**

"The only thing that overcomes hard luck is hard work." - Harry Golden

**189.**

"Goodness and hard work are rewarded with respect." - Luther Campbell

**190.**

"When I meet successful people, I ask about 100 questions to find out who they attribute their success to. It is usually the same: persistence, hard work, and hiring good people." - Kiana Tom

**191.**

"If your dream is a big dream and if you want your life to work on the high level that you say you do, there's no way around doing the work it takes to get you there." - Joyce Chapman

**192.**

"There are no shortcuts to any place worth going." - Beverly Sills

**193.**

"Hard work without talent is a shame, but talent without hard work is a tragedy." - Robert Hall

**194.**

"Inspiration is the windfall from hard work and focus. Muses are too unreliable to keep on the payroll." - Helen Hanson

**195.**

"Do the things you like to be happier, stronger, and more successful. Only so is hard work replaced by dedication." - Rossana Condoleo

**196.**

"Once you have commitment, you need the discipline and hard work to get you there." – Haile Gebrselassie

**197.**

"Start by doing what's necessary, and then what's possible; and suddenly you are doing the impossible." - Saint Francis

**198.**

"People are like stained glass windows, they sparkle and shine when the sun is out, but when darkness sets in, and their true beauty is revealed only if there is a light from within." - Elisabeth Kubler Ross

**199.**

"With the new day comes new strength and new thoughts" - Eleanor Roosevelt

**200.**

"It's hard to wait around for something you know might never happen, but it's harder to give up when you know it's everything you want." - Unknown

**201.**

"Go for the moon. If you don't get it, you'll still be heading for a star. Happiness lies not in the mere possession of money; it lies in the joy of achievement, in the thrill of the creative effort." - Franklin Delano Roosevelt

**202.**

"It always seems impossible until it's done." - Nelson Mandela

**203.**

"Set your goals high, and don't stop till you get there." - Bo Jackson

**204.**

"We have to allow ourselves to be loved by the people who really love us, the people who really matter. Too much of the time, we are blinded by our own pursuits of people to love us, people that don't even matter, while all that time we waste and the people who do love us have to stand on the sidewalk and watch us beg in the streets! It's time to put an end to this. It's time for us to let ourselves be loved." - C. JoyBell C.

**205.**

"If you're not stubborn, you'll give up on experiments too soon. And if you're not flexible, you'll pound your head against the wall and you won't see a different solution to a problem you're trying to solve." - Jeff Bezos

**206.**

"Our greatest weakness lies in giving up. The most certain way to succeed is always to try just one more time."- Thomas Edison

**207.**

"Problems are not stop signs; they are guidelines" - Robert H. Schuller

**208.**

"Without hard work, nothing grows but weeds." - Gordon B. Hinckley

**209.**

"If you fell down yesterday, stand up today." - H. G. Wells

**210.**

"Keep your eyes on the stars and your feet on the ground." - Theodore Roosevelt

**211.**

"Definiteness of purpose is the starting point of all achievement." - W. Clement Stone

**212.**

"Nearly all men can stand adversity, but if you want to test a man's character, give him power." - Abraham Lincoln

**213.**

"I can, therefore, I am." - Simone Weil

**214.**

"Quality is not an act, it is a habit."- Aristotle

**215.**

"If your actions inspire others to dream more, learn more, do more and become more, you are a leader." - John Quincy Adams

**216.**

"What you do today can improve all your tomorrows." - Ralph Marston.

**217.**

"The key is to keep company only with people who uplift you, whose presence calls forth your best." - Epictetus

**218.**

"Do not go where the path may lead, go instead where there is no path and leave a trail." - Ralph Waldo Emerson

**219.**

"There is only one corner of the universe you can be certain of improving and that's your own self."- Aldous Huxley

**220.**

"Look up at the stars and not down at your feet. Try to make sense of what you see, and wonder what makes the universe exist. Be curious." - Stephen Hawking

**221.**

"When something is important enough, you do it even if the odds are not in your favor." - Elon Musk

**222.**

"If we all did the things we are capable of doing, we could literally astound ourselves." - Thomas Alva Edison

**223.**

"Success is going from failure to failure without losing your enthusiasm." -Winston Churchill

**224.**

"Sometimes, you can't see yourself clearly until you see yourself through the eyes of others." - Ellen DeGeneres

**225.**

"The will to succeed is important, but what's more important is the will to prepare." - Bobby Knight

**226.**

"Twenty years from now, you will be more disappointed by the things you didn't do than by the ones you did do. So throw off the bowlines. Sail away from the safe harbor. Catch the trade winds in your sail. Explore. Dream. Discover." - Mark Twain

**227.**

"Take chances, make mistakes. That's how you grow. Pain nourishes your courage. You have to fail in order to practice being brave." - Mary Tyler Moore

**228.**

"We can each define ambition and progress for ourselves. The goal is to work toward a world where expectations are not set by the stereotypes that hold us back, but by our personal passion, talents, and interests." - Sheryl Sandberg

**229.**

"Don't be afraid to be ambitious about your goals. Hard work never stops. Neither should your dreams."- Dwayne Johnson

**230.**

"The purpose of life, after all, is to live it. To taste experience to the utmost, to reach out eagerly and without fear for newer and richer experience." - Eleanor Roosevelt

**231.**

"Ambition is a dream with a V8 engine." - Elvis Presley

**232.**

"The secret of making dreams come true can be summarized in four C's. They are curiosity, confidence, courage, and constancy; and the greatest of these is confidence." - Walt Disney

**233.**

"If your actions create a legacy that inspires others to dream more, learn more, do more, and become more, then you are an excellent leader." - Dolly Parton

**234.**

"The secret of change is to focus all of your energy not on fighting the old but on building the new." - Socrates

**235.**

"Make up your mind that no matter what comes your way, no matter how difficult, no matter how unfair, you will do more than simply survive. You will thrive in spite of it all." - Joel Osteen

**236.**

"The most powerful, efficient energy source in the world is your own mind. Explore and discover that it can make creative fuel from anything." - Bruce Garrabrandt

**237.**

"Our uniqueness, our individuality, and our life experience mold us into fascinating beings. I pray we may all challenge ourselves to delve into the deepest resources of our hearts to cultivate an atmosphere of understanding, acceptance, tolerance, and compassion. We are all in this life together." - Linda Thompson

**238.**

"To be courageous requires exceptional qualifications, no magic formula. It's an opportunity that sooner or later is presented to us all and each person must look for that courage in their own soul." - John F. Kennedy

**239.**

"Having a positive mental attitude is asking how something can be done rather than saying it can't be done." - Bo Bennett

**240.**

"The person who sends out positive thoughts activates the world around him positively and draws back to himself positive results." - Norman Vincent Peale

**241.**

"Just smiling goes a long way toward making you feel better about life. And when you feel better about life, your life is better. With an optimistic, positive attitude toward life, the possibilities for your second prime are tremendous." - Art Linkletter

**242.**

"The most difficult thing is the decision to act, the rest is merely tenacity." - Amelia Earhart

**243.**

"There are only two ways to live your life. One is as though nothing is a miracle. The other is as though everything is a miracle." - Albert Einstein

**244.**

"What we think, we become. All that we are arises with our thoughts. With our thoughts, we make the world." - Buddha

**245.**

"To go against the dominant thinking of your friends, of most of the people you see every day, is perhaps the most difficult act of heroism you can perform." - Theodore H. White

**246.**

"When we quit thinking primarily about ourselves and our own self-preservation, we undergo a truly heroic transformation of consciousness." - Joseph Campbell

**247.**

"Always remember you are braver than you believe, stronger than you seem, and smarter than you think." - Christopher Robin

**248.**

"The best time to plant a tree was 20 years ago. The second best time is now." - Chinese Proverb

**249.**

"Fall seven times and stand up eight." - Japanese Proverb

**250.**

"Welcome every morning with a smile. Look on the new day as another special gift from your creator, another golden opportunity to complete what you were unable to finish yesterday. Be a self-starter. Let your first hour set the theme of success and positive action that is certain to echo through your entire day. Today will never happen again. Don't waste with a false start or no start at all. You were not born to fail." - Og Mandino

**251.**

"When we create something, we always create it first in a thought form. If we are basically positive in attitude, expecting and envisioning pleasure, satisfaction, and happiness, we will attract and create people, situation, and events which conform to our positive expectation." - Shakti Gawain

**252.**

"A positive attitude may not solve every problem but it makes solving any problem a more pleasant experience." - Grant Fairley

**253.**

"Like success, failure is many things to many people. With a positive mental attitude, failure is a learning experience, a rung on the ladder, a plateau at which to get your thoughts in order and prepare to try again" - W. Clement Stone

**254.**

"People deal too much with the negative, with what is wrong...why not try and see positive things, to just touch those things and make them bloom?" - Thich Nhat Hanh

**255.**

"Don't be discouraged by a failure. It can be a positive experience. Failure is, in a sense, the highway to success, in as much as every discovery of what is false leads us to seek earnestly after what is true, and every fresh experience points out some."- John Keats

**256.**

"With courage, you will dare to take risks, have the strength to be compassionate, and the wisdom to be humble. Courage is the foundation of integrity." - Keshavan Nair

**257.**

"Courage is what it takes to stand up and speak; courage is also what it takes to sit down and listen." - Winston Churchill

**258.**

"If you want to be happy, set a goal that commands your thoughts, liberates your energy, and inspires your hopes." - Andrew Carnegie

**259.**

"You are your master. Only you have the master keys to open the inner locks." - Amit Ray

**260.**

"Live boldly. Laugh loudly. Love truly. Play as often as you can. Work as smart as you are able. Share your heart as deeply as you can reach."- Mary Anne Radmacher

**261.**

"The beauty of facing life unprepared is tremendous. Then life has a newness, a youth; then life has a flow and freshness. Then life has so many surprises. And when life has so many surprises, boredom never settles in you."- Osho

**262.**

"Success is not measured by what you accomplish, but by the opposition you have encountered, and the courage with which you have maintained the struggle against overwhelming odds." - Orison Swett Marden

**263.**

"I act with bold courage – taking inspiration from the powerful vision of my future, I boldly set sail with courage and intent. I hold my course with focused attention and relentless commitment, as I weather the storms of life." - Jonathan Lockwood Huie

**264.**

"You have power over your mind- not outside events. Realize this, and you will find strength."- Marcus Aurelius

**265.**

"Honor your being, release each and every struggle, gather strength from life's storms, and relax into the arms of spirit." - Johnathan Lockwood Huie

**266.**

"It's being willing to walk away that gives you strength and power – if you're willing to accept the consequences of doing what you want to do." - Whoopi Goldberg

**267.**

"Our deepest fear is not that we are inadequate. Our deepest fear is that we are powerful beyond measure. It is our light, not our darkness, that most frightens us." - Marianne Williamson

**268.**

"When the power of love overcomes the love of power, the world will know peace." - Jimi Hendrix

**269.**

"Hard work keeps the wrinkles out of the mind and spirit." - Helena Rubinstein

**270.**

"The best way to not feel hopeless is to get up and do something. Don't wait for good things to happen to you. If you go out and make some good things happen, you will fill the world with hope, you will fill yourself with hope."
- Barack Obama

**271.**

"Live with intention. Walk to the edge. Listen hard. Practice wellness. Play with abandon. Laugh. Choose with no regret. Appreciate your friends. Continue to learn. Do what you love. Live as if there is all there is." - Mary Anne Radmacher

**272.**

"A pessimist sees the difficulty in every opportunity; an optimist sees the opportunity in every difficulty" - Sir Winston Churchill

**273.**

"I am determined to be cheerful and happy in whatever situation I may find myself. For I have learned that the greater part of our misery or unhappiness is determined not by our circumstance but by our disposition." - Martha Washington

**274.**

"There will come a time when you believe everything is finished. That will be the beginning." - Louis L'Amour

**275.**

"Change your life today. Don't gamble on the future, act now, without delay." - Simone de Beauvoir

**276.**

"The best and most beautiful things in the world cannot be seen or even touched. They must be felt with the heart." -Helen Keller

**277.**

"I've missed more than 9,000 shots in my career. I've lost almost 300 games. 26 times I've been trusted to take the game winning shot and missed. I've failed over and over and over again in my life. And that is why I succeed." - Michael Jordan

**278.**

"Life is a song – sing it. Life is a game – play it. Life is a challenge – meet it. Life is a dream – realize it. Life is a sacrifice – offer it. Life is love – enjoy it."- Sai Baba

**279.**

"Make your life a masterpiece; imagine no limitations on what you can be, have or do." - Brian Tracy

**280.**

"If you love what you do and are willing to do what it takes, it's within your reach. And it'll be worth every minute you spend alone at night, thinking and thinking about what it is you want to design or build."
- Steve Wozniak

**281.**

"The best remedy for those who are afraid, lonely or unhappy is to go outside, somewhere where they can be quiet, alone with the heavens, nature, and God. Because only then does one feel that all is as it should be." - Anne Frank

**282.**

"Nothing is impossible, the word itself says, "I'm possible!" - Audrey Hepburn

**283.**

"Pride is holding your head up when everyone around you has theirs bowed. Courage is what makes you do it." - Bryce Courtenay

**284.**

"Take time to laugh at yourself. Those who feel too important to laugh at themselves rob themselves, their family, and their friends of a great source of joy. The most wasted of all days is one without laughter."
- E E Cummings

**285.**

"Laugh at yourself and at life. Not in the spirit of derision of whining self-pity, but as a remedy, a miracle drug, that will ease your pain, cure your depression, and help you to put in perspective that seemingly terrible defeat and worry with laughter at your predicaments, thus freeing your mind to think clearly toward the solution that is certain to come. Never take yourself too seriously." - Og Mandino

**286.**

"I will not play tug o' war. I'd rather play hug o' war. Where everyone hugs instead of tugs, where everyone giggles and rolls on the rug, where everyone kisses and everyone grins, and everyone cuddles and everyone wins."- Shel Silverstein.

**287.**

"It is our choices...that show what we truly are, far more than our abilities." - J. K. Rowling

**288.**

"May your life always be a counterpoint to the clamor of the world. May your delight in dancing lightly with life. May you soar on eagle wings, high above the madness of the world. May you always sing melody in the symphony of your life. May you taste, smell, and touch your dreams of a beautiful tomorrow. May your sun always shine, and your sky be forever blue." - Jonathan Lockwood Huie

**289.**

"Always be yourself and have faith in yourself. Do not go out and look for a successful personality and try to duplicate it." - Bruce Lee

**290.**

"Find a time and place of solitude. Look into the distance, and into the future. Visualize the tomorrow you are going to build – and begin to build that tomorrow, today." - Jonathan Lockwood Huie

**291.**

"Leadership is not magnetic personality - that can just as well be a glib tongue. It is not 'making friends and influencing people' - that is flattery. Leadership is lifting a person's vision to high sights, the raising of a person's performance to a higher standard, the building of a personality beyond its normal limitations."–Peter F. Drucker

**292.**

"I receive all of life with thanksgiving – I have gratitude for everything that has occurred to bring me to this moment. I give thanks for the joys and the sufferings, the moments of peace and the flashes of anger, the compassion and the indifference, the roar of my courage and the cold sweat of my fear. I accept gratefully the entirety of my past and my present life." - Jonathan Lockwood Huie

**293.**

"Do you really want to look back on your life and see how wonderful it could have been had you not been afraid to live it?" - Caroline Myss

**294.**

"Don't be trapped by dogma – which is living with the results of other people's thinking. Don't let the noise of other's opinions drown out your own inner voice." - Steve Jobs

**295.**

"Trust your own inner guidance. Have faith that your steps are carrying you toward your dreams. Keep your eyes on the heavens and believe that your feet will carry you well." - Jonathan Lockwood Huie

**296.**

"Good, better, best. Never let it rest. 'Till your good is better and your better is best."- St. Jerome

**297.**

"We're so engaged in doing things to achieve purposes of outer value that we forget the inner value, the rapture that is associated with being alive, is what it is all about." - Joseph Campbell

**298.**

"Always believe in yourself and always stretch yourself beyond your limits. Your life is worth a lot more than you think because you are capable of accomplishing more than you know. You have more potential than you think, but you will never know your full potential unless you keep challenging yourself and pushing beyond your own self-imposed limits."- Roy T. Bennett

**299.**

"Whatever you do, you need courage. Whatever course you decide upon, there is always someone to tell you that you are wrong. There are always difficulties arising that tempt you to believe your critics are right."- Ralph Waldo Emerson

**300.**

"If you can't fly, then run; if you can't run, then walk; if you can't walk, then crawl; but whatever you do, you have to keep moving forward." – Dr. Martin Luther King Jr.

**301.**

"Maybe you can afford to wait. Maybe for you, there's a tomorrow. Maybe for you, there's one thousand tomorrows, or three thousand, or ten, so much time you can bathe in it, roll around it, and let it slide like coins through your fingers. So much time you can waste it. But for some of us, there's only today. And the truth is, you never really know."- Lauren Oliver

**302.**

"I have realized; it is during the times I am far outside my element that I experience myself the most. That I see and feel who I really am the most! I think that's what a comet is like, you see, a comet is born in the outer realms of the universe! But it's only when it ventures too close to our sun or to other stars that it releases the blazing "tail" behind it and shoots brazen through the heavens! And meteors become sucked into our atmosphere before they burst like firecrackers and realize that they're shooting stars! That's why I enjoy taking myself out of my own element, my own comfort zone, and hurling myself out into the unknown. Because it's during those scary moments, those unsure steps taken, that I am able to see that I'm like a comet hitting a new atmosphere: suddenly, I illuminate magnificently and fire dust begin to fall off of me! I discover a smile I didn't know I had, I uncover a feeling that I didn't know existed in me... I see myself. I'm a shooting star. A meteor shower. But I'm not going to die out. I guess I'm more like a comet then. I'm just going to keep on coming back." - C. JoyBell C.

**303.**

"Fake it until you make it! Act as if you had all the confidence you require until it becomes your reality."
- Brian Tracy

**304.**

"Excellence is an art won by training and habituation. We do not act rightly because we have virtue or excellence, but we rather have those because we have acted rightly. We are what we repeatedly do. Excellence, then, is not an act but a habit."–Aristotle

**305.**

"The great thing in this world is not so much where you stand, as in what direction you are moving." - Oliver Wendell Holmes

**306.**

"We may encounter many defeats but we must not be defeated."- Maya Angelou

**307.**

"The highest reward for man's toil is not what he gets for it, but what he becomes by it." - John Ruskin

**308.**

"Nothing in the world can take the place of Persistence. Talent will not; nothing is more common than unsuccessful men with talent. Genius will not; unrewarded genius is almost a proverb. Education will not; the world is full of educated derelicts. Persistence and determination alone are omnipotent. The slogan 'Press On' has solved and always will solve the problems of the human race."–Calvin Coolidge

**309.**

"All of the great leaders have had one characteristic in common: it was the willingness to confront unequivocally the major anxiety of their people in their time. This, and not much else, is the essence of leadership."–John Kenneth Galbraith

**310.**

"The most dangerous leadership myth is that leaders are born - that there is a genetic factor to leadership. This myth asserts that people simply either have certain charismatic qualities or not. That's nonsense; in fact, the opposite is true. Leaders are made rather than born."–Warren G. Bennis

**311.**

"The winners in life think constantly in terms of I can, I will, and I am. Losers, on the other hand, concentrate their waking thoughts on what they should have or would have done, or what they can't do." - Dennis Waitley

**312.**

"Appreciate again and again, freshly and naively, the basic goods of life, with awe, pleasure, wonder, and even ecstasy, however stale these experiences may have become to others." - Abraham Maslow

**313.**

"We should not give up and we should not allow the problem to defeat us." - A. P. J. Abdul Kalam

**314.**

"It is a paradoxical but profoundly true and important principle of life that the most likely way to reach a goal is to be aiming not at that goal itself but at some more ambitious goal beyond it."–Arnold Toynbee

**315.**

"The great successful men of the world have used their imagination. They think ahead and create their mental picture in all its details, filling in here, adding a little there, altering this a bit and that a bit, but steadily building – steadily building."–Robert Collier

**316.**

"Far better is it to dare mighty things, to win glorious triumphs – even though checkered by failure – than to rank with those poor spirits who neither enjoy much nor suffer much, because they live in a gray twilight that knows not victory nor defeat." - Theodore Roosevelt

**317.**

"Accept responsibility for your life. Know that it is you who will get you where you want to go, no one else."- Les Brown

**318.**

"Just know, when you truly want success, you'll never give up on it. No matter how bad the situation may get."- Unknown

**319.**

"We may encounter many defeats but we must not be defeated." - Maya Angelou

**320.**

"Happiness cannot be traveled to, owned, earned, or worn. It is the spiritual experience of living every minute with love, grace, and gratitude." - Denis Waitley

**321.**

"Challenges are what make life interesting and overcoming them is what makes life meaningful." - Joshua J. Marine

**322.**

"Dream big and dare to fail." - Norman Vaughan

**323.**

"Beginning today, treat everyone you meet as if they were going to be dead by midnight. Extend to them all the care, kindness, and understanding you can muster, and do it with no thought of any reward. Your life will never be the same again."- Og Mandino

**324.**

"Courage is grace under pressure." - Ernest Hemingway

**325.**

"As soon as you trust yourself, you will know how to live." - Johann Wolfgang von Goethe

**326.**

"Someone is sitting in the shade today because someone planted a tree a long time ago." - Warren Buffett

**327.**

"There is no easy walk to freedom anywhere, and many of us will have to pass through the valley of the shadow of death again and again before we reach the mountaintop of our desires." - Nelson Mandela

**328.**

"The difference between winning and losing is most often not quitting."
- Walt Disney

**329.**

"If there is no struggle, there is no progress." - Frederick Douglass

**330.**

"Talk to yourself like you would to someone you love." - Brene Brown

**331.**

"You can't please everyone, and you can't make everyone like you." - Katie Couric

**332.**

"The longer I live, the more beautiful life becomes." - Frank Lloyd Wright

**333.**

"Don't limit yourself. Many people limit themselves to what they think they can do. You can go as far as your mind lets you. What you believe, remember, you can achieve." - Mary Kay Ash

**334.**

"I think that the power is the principle. The principle of moving forward, as though you have the confidence to move forward, eventually gives you confidence when you look back and see what you've done." - Robert Downey Jr.

**335.**

"As you grow older, you will discover that you have two hands, one for helping yourself, the other for helping others." - Audrey Hepburn

**336.**

"It often requires more courage to dare to do right than to fear to do wrong." - Abraham Lincoln

**337.**

"The biggest risk is not taking any risk... In a world that's changing really quickly, the only strategy that is guaranteed to fail is not taking risks." - Mark Zuckerberg

**338.**

"Identity is a prison you can never escape, but the way to redeem your past is not to run from it, but to try to understand it, and use it as a foundation to grow." - Jay-Z

**339.**

"Don't count the days, make the days count." - Muhammad Ali

**340.**

"Change will not come if we wait for some other person or some other time. We are the ones we've been waiting for. We are the change that we seek." - Barack Obama

**341.**

"Everything you can imagine is real." - Pablo Picasso

**342.**

"Life is short, and it is here to be lived." - Kate Winslet

**343.**

"Do the difficult things while they are easy and do the great things while they are small. A journey of a thousand miles must begin with a single step." - Lao Tzu

**344.**

"In the midst of movement and chaos, keep stillness inside of you." - Deepak Chopra

**345.**

"Try to be a rainbow in someone's cloud." - Maya Angelou

**346.**

"We should remember that just as a positive outlook on life can promote good health, so can everyday acts of kindness." - Hillary Clinton

**347.**

"Be yourself. Everyone else is already taken." - Oscar Wilde

**348.**

"There are no mistakes, only opportunities." - Tina Fey

**349.**

"Security is mostly a superstition. It does not exist in nature, nor do the children of men as a whole experience it. Avoiding danger is no safer in the long run than outright exposure. Life is either a daring adventure or nothing." - Helen Keller

**350.**

"In the middle of every difficulty lies opportunity." - Albert Einstein

**351.**

"Don't be distracted by criticism. Remember – the only taste of success some people get is to take a bite out of you." - Zig Ziglar

**352.**

"But you have to do what you dream of doing even while you're afraid." - Arianna Huffington

**353.**

"Success isn't about how much money you make. It's about the difference you make in people's lives." - Michelle Obama

**354.**

"If you can do what you do best and be happy, you're further along in life than most people." - Leonardo DiCaprio

**355.**

"Don't let the fear of striking out hold you back." - Babe Ruth

**356.**

"Infuse your life with action. Don't wait for it to happen. Make it happen. Make your own future. Make your own hope. Make your own love and whatever your beliefs, honor your creator, not by passively waiting for grace to come down from upon high but by doing what you can to make grace happen...yourself, right now, right down here on Earth."-Bradley Whitford

**357.**

"Life isn't about finding yourself. Life is about creating yourself." - George Bernard Shaw

**358.**

"If you live long enough, you'll make mistakes. But if you learn from them, you'll be a better person." - Bill Clinton

**359.**

"What the mind of man can conceive and believe, it can achieve." - Napoleon Hill

**360.**

"As long as the mind can envision the fact that you can do something, you can do it, as long as you really believe 100 percent." - Arnold Schwarzenegger

**361.**

"Start where you are. Use what you have. Do what you can." - Arthur Ashe

**362.**

"Find out who you are and be that person. That's what your soul was put on this Earth to be. Find that truth, live that truth, and everything else will come." - Ellen DeGeneres

**363.**

"The way I see it, if you want the rainbow, you gotta put up with the rain." - Dolly Parton

**364.**

"To dream the impossible dream... and the world will be better for this that one man, scorned and cover with scars, still strove with his last ounce of courage to reach the unreachable star." - Joe Darion (Man of La Mancha)

**365.**

"All things share the same breath – the beast, the tree, the man... the air shares its spirit with all the life it supports." - Chief Seattle

# Conclusion

Thank you for making it through to the end of *365 Positive Thinking Quotes*. Let's hope it was informative and able to provide you with all of the tools you need to achieve your goals whatever they may be.

The next step is to read all of these quotes and motivate yourself to do better each day! Each quote is going to help you start out your day in a positive manner so you do not have to stress first thing in the morning. Starting your day out positive will help you to be motivated to keep your day positive!

Finally, if you found this book useful in any way, a review on Amazon is always appreciated!

Thank you and good luck!

*Ben L Orchard*

CPSIA information can be obtained
at www.ICGtesting.com
Printed in the USA
BVHW041659200323
660798BV00017B/371